FREQUENCY

STUDY GUIDE

FOR GROUP DISCUSSION
AND PERSONAL REFLECTION

FREQUENCY

STUDY GUIDE

FOR GROUP DISCUSSION AND PERSONAL REFLECTION

ROBERT MORRIS

We hope you hear from the Holy Spirit and receive God's richest blessings from this book by Gateway Press. We want to provide the highest quality resources that take the messages, music, and media of Gateway Church to the world. For more information on other resources from Gateway Publishing, go to gatewaypublishing.com.

ISBN: 978-1-945529-13-9
First Edition Printed 2017

Gateway Press, an imprint of Gateway Publishing
700 Blessed Way
Southlake, Texas 76092
www.gatewaypublishing.com

CONTENTS

CHAPTER ONE

THE BEAUTY
OF BEING SHEEP

Key Thought

According to God's Word, He is the Great Shepherd, we are His sheep, and His sheep hear His voice. We are born with an innate ability to hear God, but we must learn and mature in our ability to hear Him.

Summary

Jesus calls us into a close relationship with Him, where we instantly recognize His voice. The God of the universe invites us to enjoy a familiar relationship with Him, one in which we pray to Him and He listens to us, and He speaks to us and we listen to Him. God wants us to grasp a foundational truth that He wants to talk to us in the first place. You need to grab hold of that amazing truth. He wants us to live in such a way that we don't simply depend primarily on our pastor's teaching, our conscience, or a church service each week, but instead that we live by God's voice. However, often many Christians are unfamiliar with the concept of living by the voice of God.

What is the main difference between a believer and an unbeliever? It is that a believer has a personal relationship with God. There is a difference between having a personal relationship with God and having an impersonal religion where you only know facts about God. Paul writes about a personal relationship with God (Ephesians 5:22–33). Any personal relationship requires communication. If true dialogue and communication don't take place, then the relationship is not personal.

The Bible contains many examples of God speaking to His people. God talks in the very beginning with Adam and Eve. Throughout both Testaments, God speaks. He communicated with people over thousands of years of recorded history, and He has not changed. God did not become mute. He still speaks to us today, just as He has spoken to His people throughout history.

Jesus calls Himself the Good Shepherd, and contrasts His work with that of Satan, who is a thief and a robber (John 10). Jesus calls us sheep. He says specifically that His sheep hear His voice. Not only that, but because they know His voice, they follow Him and not another. Jesus describes how we are to live. We are to listen to His voice. When we hear Jesus' voice, we will follow Him.

Our ability to hear God is innate. When we were born again and became came alive in Christ, we received the ability to hear God. We became spiritual sheep who can hear the Good Shepherd.

Our ability to hear God is not only innate, but it is also learned. In the same way that we have an innate ability to pray, we also need to learn how to pray. We must grow in our understanding of how to hear God. Our children are born with the ability to communicate, but we still need to teach them how to speak and listen. We are born with many abilities, but we must learn to use them through practice. Hearing God is the same. Someone who has spent hours in prayer and listening to God, and has walked with the Lord for years, will have a greater ability to hear God than someone who is a new believer. Don't be discouraged if you feel like you can't hear God the same way as someone else. You can learn to hear God's voice. Remember, you are a sheep and He is the Good Shepherd.

Our ability to hear God can mature. Just as children learn to communicate better as they become older, you can learn how to hear God better over time. We can all learn how God speaks to us and then mature in our ability to communicate. For example, sometimes people think they are hearing God, when they are merely repeating things that come from their religious backgrounds.

Sometimes people act as if they continually hear a stream of God talking to them all the time. These people receive "a message a minute." Generally, this type of behavior comes from someone who has an immature understanding, desires unnecessary attention, or simply made a mistake. However, everything from God comes into alignment with Scripture. As parents, we know that we communicate with our children, but we don't barrage them with a constant stream of talking without taking a breath.

We should also be careful of people who say they have a "can't-fail" method or formula for hearing God's voice. Hearing God comes about because we have a real relationship with Him. We don't need to be mystical or weird to hear God. The Bible contains many examples of both the general will of God, which is for everyone, and the specific will of God. The general will of God includes elements such as the Great Commission (Matthew 18:19–20), being conformed to the image of God's Son (Romans 8:28–29), and other things that tell us how to live as Christians. The specific will of God includes times when God reveals His will specifically or individually to a person. For example, God spoke directly to Abraham, Moses, and Paul. Just as God guided His servants in specific manners in the past, He also guides His servants today. God designed us to hear his voice so that we can grow and mature in our ability to hear Him speak to us.

Group Opener

How do you make decisions? Are you a deep thinker, do you list the pros and cons, or do you "go with your gut"?

Group Talk

1. Did you grow up with the idea that hearing God is normal, or was it a strange or awkward concept?

. . . .
. . . .
. . . .

2. One of the most common questions that I receive is "How can I hear God?" Why do you think people are so eager to get the answer to this question?

. . . .
. . . .
. . . .

3. The Scripture says that Jesus is the Good Shepherd, you are one of His sheep, and His sheep hear His voice. How does that make you feel?

. . . .
. . . .
. . . .

4. What are some things that you have learned and have grown to do better over time, such as hobbies, vocational skills, etc.? How does this same principle of learning and maturing apply to hearing God's voice?

. . . .
. . . .
. . . .

5. Can you think of a time in your life when you've heard God's voice? What did God say and how did you respond? What was the result?

. . . .
. . . .
. . . .

Prayer

Heavenly Father, thank You for making us with the innate ability to hear Your voice. We love having a personal relationship with You, and we are thankful that You speak to us. Please teach us to hear Your voice more clearly. Help us to mature in our ability to hear You and how to respond. In Jesus name, Amen.

Explore

Want to go deeper? Here's some food for thought, prayer, and journaling for the next week.

Key Quote

So a personal relationship must involve communication—it must.

—Robert Morris

- If communication was only one-sided and one person never spoke, how would you describe that relationship?

....
....
....

- How does it make you feel to know that God wants to speak to you because He wants to have a personal relationship with you?

....
....
....

Key Scripture

But he who enters by the door is the shepherd of the sheep. To him the doorkeeper opens, and the sheep hear his voice; and he calls his own sheep by name and leads them out. And when he brings out his own sheep, he goes before them; and the sheep follow him, for they know his voice. Yet they will by no means follow a stranger, but will flee from him, for they do not know the voice of strangers (John 10:2–5).

As you read these verses, what is the Holy Spirit saying to you?

. . . .

. . . .

. . . .

Key Questions

1. How does the concept of hearing God make you feel? Does it go against any religious teaching from your past?

. . . .

. . . .

. . . .

2. What does it mean to you to live by God's voice? How would your life change if you listened for God more carefully?

. . . .

. . . .

. . . .

Key Responses

1. This week, read in your Bible about people who have heard God's voice. As you read, watch specifically for what it looked like for them when they heard God. Write down some of the various ways God has spoken to people since the beginning of creation.

. . . .
. . . .
. . . .

2. The Bible says to ask and you will receive. Whether you want to hear God for the first time, learn to hear Him better, or mature in your current ability to hear Him—ask God to help you to hear Him more clearly. Ask Him to teach you. He will.

. . . .
. . . .
. . . .

CHAPTER TWO

WHY HEAR FROM GOD?

Key Thought

God speaks to us because He desires relationship with us. He wants to be our friend. God does not speak to us mechanically, but He speaks to us as a friend.

Summary

God desires a deep, rich relationship with us. Often, we approach God as if He is a great cosmic Santa Claus. We're distant and removed, and our only motive is to get something from Him. We only want to receive blessing, direction, or instruction from Him. Yet God wants something far greater than that. He wants to get to know us, and He desires for us to get to know Him.

The doctrine of *transcendence* means that God is superior, immense, and unequaled—higher than anything we can think or imagine. While this is an accurate doctrine, some people have allowed it to keep them from having a deep relationship with God because they don't also understand the doctrine of *immanence*. This doctrine means that God is close to us; He is Immanuel—"God with us." From these two foundational doctrines, God invites us into a true friendship with Him. We should keep in mind the greatness of the Person to whom we're talking and relating. However, Jesus also clearly says, "No longer do I call you servants, for a servant does not know what his master is doing; but I have called you friends, for all things that I heard from My Father I have made known to you" (John 15:15).

God didn't design us to obey His commands mindlessly. He created us with souls, minds, wills, emotions, and hearts. God wants to communicate with us personally, because He gave us personalities. He did not create us as robots. Instead, God made us as His children. In a personal way, God communicates with the children He created. He called Abraham His friend, which established an example for how we should communicate with God. Abraham drew near to the Lord and spoke to Him respectfully, but also as a friend. When Abraham found out about God's plan to destroy Sodom and Gomorrah, he engaged God in conversation. Abraham acknowledged that God is a God of justice, but he also knew that God cares about the people. Abraham's respectful conversation began by asking God to consider sparing the city if there were fifty righteous people in it. When God showed His mercy in His response that He would spare the city, the conversation continued. God invites us into this type of prayer. As Abraham talked with God, it was relational. Abraham acknowledged God's character and interceded for the people.

God speaks to people. He spoke to people in the Bible, and He still speaks today. God spoke in many different ways in the Scriptures. He speaks to people because He cares about them. God constantly speaks to people, always inviting them to draw a step closer to Him. He speaks to us today because the Holy Spirit indwells us. Jesus says that the Holy Spirit will speak to us and tell us what He hears (John 16).

Sometimes, we have the idea that God spoke in the Bible through a big booming voice. Occasionally, God spoke this way, such as when He spoke to Jesus and people thought it thundered, but He did not speak that way all the time. When God spoke to Elijah in the wilderness, He used a still small voice, more like a gentle whisper than a clap of thunder. When the Holy Spirit speaks today, we don't have to look for a booming audible sound, but rather we listen to His still small voice speaking in our heart. God did not speak to Gideon in a loud audible voice. Gideon felt uncertain, so he asked God for several confirmations. In Hebrews 11, the "hall of faith" chapter, the author lists the people who heard from God, but still had to live by faith. Often, when God speaks to us through His still small voice, we still have to live out that word by faith.

God also speaks to people as friends. We read in Exodus, "So the Lord spoke to Moses face to face, as a man speaks to his friend" (Exodus 33:11). God wants to be our friend in the same way He was the friend of Moses. Friendship with God is an incredible privilege and a responsibility. Friendship with God is at the core of the gospel message. Jesus said that He lays down His life for His friends, and He laid down His life for us. We have no formalities with our earthly best friends. We have no fear, nor do we communicate with rituals or special language. A deep, close relationship is intimate and personal. God speaks to us because He wants to be our friend. He designed us to communicate with Him on a personal level and in a personal way.

My son, James, spend the day fishing alone when he was younger, and he caught many fish. This was a great day for James, because he loves fishing. The next day, I joined him for a day of fishing, but we didn't catch any fish. When I apologized to him that it wasn't as good a day as the previous day, James replied, "Dad, today was much better than yesterday because you were here with me." That is what it is like between God and us. God simply loves to be with us. Often, we bring our lists and requests to God. That is the right thing to do sometimes, because the Bible does say to cast our cares upon Him. However, God simply wants to be with us, even more than listening to our requests. He wants to commune with us as friends.

Group Opener

What is the funniest or most adventurous thing you've ever done with a friend?

Group Talk

1. Think about your closest friend. How do you communicate and talk together? How did the quality of your communication grow over time?

. . . .
. . . .
. . . .

2. What would you say are the qualities of a good friend? In what ways does God show those qualities to us? In what ways do you show those qualities to Him?

. . . .
. . . .
. . . .

3. What would it look like if we related to God like robots and
    we received instructions from God without a relationship?
    How would that feel?

. . . .
. . . .
. . . .

4. What do you think it means when the Bible says God speaks
    to us in a still small voice? Why do you think He does this?

. . . .
. . . .
. . . .

5. How has God made Himself known to you as a friend?

. . . .
. . . .
. . . .

Prayer

Heavenly Father, thank You for relating to us as a friend. We
recognize that You are the Creator of the Universe and more splendid
than anything we can imagine. Also, thank You for being Immanuel,
God with us. We welcome Your friendship, and we want to grow in
our relationship with You. In Jesus' name, Amen.

Explore

Want to go deeper? Here is some food for thought, prayer, and journaling in the coming week.

Key Quote

"God does not speak to robots. He speaks to people. And He speaks with people as a man speaks with his friend."

—Robert Morris

- Is it easy or difficult for you to relate to God as a friend? Why or why not?

. . . .
. . . .
. . . .

- What does it look like for you to talk with God and for Him to talk with you as a friend?

. . . .
. . . .
. . . .

Key Scripture

No longer do I call you servants, for a servant does not know what his master is doing; but I have called you friends, for all things that I heard from My Father I have made known to you (John 15:15).

As you read this verse, what is the Holy Spirit saying to you?

. . . .
. . . .
. . . .

Key Questions

1. God tells us to bring our petitions to Him and to make our requests known. He will always take care of our petitions and requests, but He also wants to sit and talk to us. Is it easy for you to sit and spend time with God, or do you usually have a list? How can you intentionally develop a healthy balance in the way you connect with God?

. . . .
. . . .
. . . .

2. What are some ways you cultivate friendships with people? What are some practical ways you can cultivate your friendship with God?

. . . .
. . . .
. . . .

Key Responses

1. When Abraham spoke with the Lord, he stopped what he was doing and drew near to God. How can you intentionally stop what you are doing, draw near to God, and listen to Him?

. . . .
. . . .
. . . .

2. Imagine sitting with God and having a conversation just as you would have with a friend. What would you talk about with Him? What things would you share and how would you share them?

. . . .

. . . .

. . . .

CHAPTER THREE

GO TO THE BIBLE

Key Thought

God speaks to us through the Bible. His Word illuminates our path and gives us wisdom for our decisions. As we learn to enter into God's presence and listen for His voice, He will speak to us specifically through His Word.

Summary

God guides us with His voice. When we need guidance, renewal, conviction, wisdom, or confirmation about something, God will lead us. He will give us a fresh vision of the way forward. As often as we need it, He will reassure us of His love and care. To connect with God and hear His voice, we need to connect with His book, the Bible. Sometimes, the world is a dark place, and it is hard to know which way to walk. God's Word brings light to our path and shows us the way we should go. The Bible provides a road map of wisdom, a wellspring of hope, and a limitless fountain of the assurance of God's love. The Holy Spirit uses the words of Scripture gently to impress upon us the truths we need to learn and follow.

The Bible also tells us about God's character, intentions, and actions and shows us how He walks, talks, and breathes. The more we read the Bible, the more we will know His ways. As we learn God's ways and acquaint ourselves with His Word, He will make our way the clearer.

If you ever feel confused about direction, then turn first to God and read the Bible. As you do, He will shed light on your path, give you wisdom for difficult decisions, and illuminate murky or dark areas. The psalmist provides this picture for us when our path is unclear: "Your word *is* a lamp to my feet and a light to my path" (Psalm 119:105). During these times, God extends an invitation to receive light from His Word. If you read, study, memorize, and meditate on God's Word, then it will overcome darkness and bring light to every area of your life.

In seasons of difficulty, it can feel as though darkness surrounds us. Sometimes we experience great losses, such as friends, relationships, marriages, investments, or health. We may feel as if we've lost direction and need to refocus our priorities. We may experience doubt, grief, or depression. In these seasons, God wants us to turn to His Word.

As we diligently read God's Word, we will experience more and more of His light. A Bible verse written thousands of years ago is still the Word of God today. The Holy Spirit can take an ancient passage to speak to us about our current situation or about a particular personal matter. Since His Word is eternal, we can still receive practical, relevant application today. The Bible can be both literal and metaphorical at the same time.

God speaks in many ways through the Bible. If we have a consistent, logical reading plan, God speaks to us faithfully. Some people have randomly opened their Bibles and received a specific word for their particular situation. Although God can do anything, this is not the best practice for ongoing study. The best method is consistent, diligent, and daily Bible reading. Sometimes, in worship or prayer, God will impress a specific Bible passage on our hearts.

When we want God to speak clearly through His Word, we should first enter into God's presence where we cultivate a deliberate awareness of His reality and nearness. Many people find a quiet place to worship God and thank Him for His faithfulness. As we connect with God and recognize His presence through praise, worship, and prayer, we can more easily lay our burdens at His feet. Sometimes writing down prayers helps our minds stay focused. Writing also helps us release our thoughts and concerns to the Lord as we transfer them from our minds, hearts, and souls onto paper. This practice also gives us a way to see the things that God has done. During these times, you may hear the whisper of the Holy Spirit and a Bible verse may come to your mind. It may be a Bible story, or a particular chapter or section. Often, the verse that comes to your mind will be exactly what you need to hear.

For example, you may pray about marriage and then purposefully read about particular marriages in the Bible or from passages specifically about marriage. Or, you may pray about finances, and then read Scriptures that relate to stewardship. These passages may not have obvious, direct application, but often God will show you how their principles apply to your life. Sometimes He will give you general direction, but you will also receive very specific, pointed messages for your current situation.

If you meet with the Lord daily and read Scripture on a regular basis, it will become easier for you to hear God. Rigid time requirements are not the goal, so give yourself enough time to really connect with God. Cultivate your time with God. The more you intentionally enter His presence, listen for clarity, and read the Bible, the more you will hear God's voice. Many people have followed this pattern, and God is extending the same invitation to you.

Group Opener

What is your favorite book and why? If you're not a reader and can't think of a book, what was your favorite story growing up?

Group Talk

1. What is your favorite Scripture verse or story in the Bible? Why is it your favorite?

. . . .
. . . .
. . . .

2. How can the Bible be both literal and metaphorical at the same time?

. . . .
. . . .
. . . .

3. What do you think a fruitful prayer life looks like? What are the benefits of having a daily prayer life, coupled with regular Bible reading?

. . . .
. . . .
. . . .

4. How do we know when God is speaking to us about a particular situation through the Bible?

. . . .
. . . .
. . . .

5. Have you ever prayed about something and then received a word from the Bible that was a direct word from God about your prayer request? If so, share the experience.

. . . .
. . . .
. . . .

Prayer

Heavenly Father, thank You for the gift of Your Word. Thank You for giving the Bible as a lamp to our feet and a light to our path. Please open our eyes so that we would see the wonderful things You want to tell us in Your Word. In Jesus' name, Amen.

Explore

Want to go deeper? Here is some food for thought, prayer, and journaling in the coming week.

Key Quote

"We live in a dark world, and we will stumble directionally unless we regularly switch on the bright light of God's Word. God's Word acts as a lamp and sheds light on the way we should go."

—Robert Morris

- Why do you think God's Word is depicted as a light? Why is this an important image?

. . . .
. . . .
. . . .

- In what area of your life do you need the light of God's Word to shine and give direction, wisdom, clarity, or hope?

. . . .
. . . .
. . . .

Key Scriptures

Your word *is* a lamp to my feet
And a light to my path (Psalm 119:105).

If any of you lacks wisdom, let him ask of God, who gives to all liberally and without reproach, and it will be given to him (James 1:5).

As you read these verses, what is the Holy Spirit saying to you?

....

....

....

Key Questions

1. How is the Bible like a roadmap for your life? What are some specific examples of how the Bible has given you direction?

....

....

....

2. Today, many GPS navigation systems tell users when they make a wrong turn. How does the Bible redirect us? When have you experienced redirection?

....

....

....

Key Responses

1. For God to speak to us through the Bible, we must read it! If you do not have a Bible reading plan, find one that works for you. Even if you can only read one or two chapters each day, start a habit of reading the Bible regularly.

....

....

....

2. God will also speak directly to you through specific verses or Bible stories. In your next quiet time, ask Him to put a Bible story or a passage of Scripture on your mind. Read it with the expectation that God will speak to you directly through His Word.

. . . .

. . . .

. . . .

CHAPTER FOUR

HEAR GOD'S VOICE THROUGH WORSHIP

Key Thought

When we worship God, we see and respond to Him for who He truly is. When we commune with God through worship, He meets and speaks with us.

Summary

God often speaks loudest and clearest to us when we are worshipping Him. When we worship God, we become aware of His presence and commune with Him. We can see and respond to God for who He truly is. Although we often equate worship with singing, it is actually so much more. We sing to connect with the greatness of who God is and then begin to worship Him from our heart. If you are seeking the Lord's heart, then focus on worshipping Him. When you set your heart and mind on God, you will find it much easier to hear Him.

During worship, God meets and speaks with us. When the Israelites first built God's tabernacle in the wilderness, He gave them many instructions for its construction. Most importantly, He said, "There I will meet with you, and I will speak with you" (Exodus 25:22). Today, just like in the Old Testament, we tabernacle with God—we meet with Him, and He dwells in us through the Holy Spirit. Meeting and speaking with someone are two different actions. You can speak to people without meeting them, such as in a phone call. You can also share the same location with someone and not speak or interact. God says that He will both meet with and speak to His people. In worship, we see God for who He truly is and receive from Him love, joy, peace, meekness, faith, healing, life, and all His goodness. He supplies what is lacking in us by His own person. He fills our needs by communing with and transforming us. When the God of the universe meets with us, He allows us to partake in all the attributes of His character. God also wants to talk with us, not merely to talk to us. Talking with a person implies that it is a conversation and not merely one-way communication. We can converse with God in a true dialogue about what is actually happening in our lives.

In times of worship, when we are meeting with God and He is speaking with us, we gain perspective. There we see how big God is and how small we are, how good God is, and how He takes away our iniquity. In God's presence, we find healing and refreshing. At times during worship, God will show you something, place a picture in your mind, speak to you through a vision, or simply give you a different point of view. When we see how big God is, we gain perspective of how small our problems may actually be. We may receive a glimpse of His glory or greatness. We may even see our own sinfulness and unworthiness and how desperately we need a savior—this revelation can serve as a catalyst for overwhelming thanksgiving and gratefulness for all Jesus did for us when He took our sin and shame on the cross. In Scripture, whenever people receive a vision of even a small part of who God is, they gain new perspective, reverence, and awe about God's greatness. In worship, we take our eyes off our problems and see how wonderful God is.

Worship emboldens and empowers us. When we worship the Lord, we look intently at Him, listen to His voice, and learn from Him, just as Moses stopped to gaze at the burning bush and set all his attention on God. When we aim to listen to the Lord in worship, we can intentionally quiet our minds and hearts and incline our ears to His direction. As we come into God's presence, it is much easier for us to listen.

Not only can we hear God's voice more clearly when we turn our hearts to Him in worship, but also when we are in His presence we can learn from Him. When God speaks to us, He wants to teach us His ways and reveal things to us. Sometimes we have an incorrect or an incomplete perspective, but when we meet with God and talk with Him, He will show us the right perspective. We can often hear God's voice more clearly in worship.

Group Opener

What is your favorite song and why? (This doesn't have to be a Christian song.) Who is your favorite singer or band and why?

Group Talk

1. What are some of your favorite worship songs? What do you like about them?

. . . .
. . . .
. . . .

2. What is the easiest way for you to enter into worship and set your focus and heart on God?

....
....
....

3. Has God ever said something significant to you while you were worshipping Him? Describe that experience.

....
....
....

4. What are some ways we can worship God that doesn't include music or songs?

....
....
....

5. What things hinder people from completely entering into worship?

....
....
....

Prayer

Heavenly Father, thank You for allowing us to come to your throne of grace and worship You. Thank you for the gift of Your presence. Help us to set our minds and our hearts on You as we acknowledge Your greatness. We want to commune with you and hear Your voice. Teach us to draw closer to You so we can experience more of Your presence. In Jesus' name, Amen.

Explore

Want to go deeper? Here is some food for thought, prayer, and journaling in the coming week.

Key Quote

If you are seeking to hear from the Lord, then I encourage you to enter a time of worship.

—Robert Morris

- Why do you think entering a time of worship will help you to hear from the Lord?

. . . .
. . . .
. . . .

- If you were honest with yourself, do you truly engage in worship, or do you just go through the motions? What would it look like for you to engage in worship with your whole heart and set all your attention on the greatness of God?

. . . .
. . . .
. . . .

Key Scripture

But we all, with unveiled face, beholding as in a mirror the glory of the Lord, are being transformed into the same image from glory to glory, just as by the Spirit of the Lord (2 Corinthians 3:18).

As you read this verse, what is the Holy Spirit saying to you?

. . . .

. . . .

Key Questions

1. How does worshipping God embolden us to walk in His ways and to follow Him? When have you had this experience in your own life?

. . . .

. . . .

2. God says that He will meet with and speak to us. Why is it significant to both meet with and speak to God? How do these work together? How does this look in your life?

. . . .

. . . .

Key Responses

1. Write down ways that you can actively cultivate a heart of worship as you meet with God. Make a plan to implement worship in your quiet times with the Lord.

. . . .

. . . .

2. How can you take worship beyond your quiet time? What are some things you can do this week to stay aware of God's nearness to you?

. . . .

. . . .

3. In this chapter, I mention several ways that God spoke to me. What are the ways God speaks to you? How does it affect your ability to hear God when you set a consistent time and place to meet with Him?

. . . .
. . . .
. . . .

4. What do you think of the pattern of meeting with God to be still and worship, pray and read, then listen and write? If you ever followed this type of pattern, what was your experience?

. . . .
. . . .
. . . .

5. Why do you think writing down what God says can be such a powerful tool for hearing God's voice? How have you used a journal previously? What benefits did you discover?

. . . .
. . . .
. . . .

Prayer

Heavenly Father, thank You for speaking to us. We value Your voice and want to hear from You. Please give us wisdom about a plan to make an appointment with You. Teach us to discern Your general and specific will for our lives. Thank You for caring about every part of our lives and for wanting to meet and speak with us. In Jesus' name, Amen.

Explore

Want to go deeper? Here is some food for thought, prayer, and journaling in the coming week.

Key Quote

If we just check in with God every six months or so whenever a big decision comes up, then we will miss out not only on knowing God's general will but also on a close, everyday friendship with God. So we must learn to value His voice, His general voice, on a regular basis if we want to hear His specific voice from time to time.

—Robert Morris

- How does consistently hearing God's general voice enable us to hear His specific voice?

. . . .
. . . .
. . . .

- What are some things God has shown you about His general will for your life? What are some specific things He has spoken to you?

. . . .
. . . .
. . . .

CHAPTER FIVE

VALUE HIS VOICE

Key Thought

It takes intentionality to value God's voice. When we set an appointment, focus our hearts on God, and write what He is saying, we will learn to discern what He is saying to us.

Summary

Learning to hear and to value God's voice is a process. God speaks to us and as we hear Him repeatedly, we learn to value His voice. God first spoke to me about planting Gateway Church in 1993 through a dream. I knew God gave the dream and spoke specifically about the numbers of people the church would impact. God told me that the church would have thirty thousand people, reach three hundred thousand people across the Dallas/Fort Worth Metroplex, reach three million people in Texas, and three hundred million people around the world. I originally found these numbers hard to comprehend, but God confirmed them several times. The next morning during my quiet time, God confirmed the dream through the story of King David, who numbered the people at three hundred thousand in Israel and thirty thousand in Judah. Although I already valued hearing God's voice, I learned to give it even more value. God will speak and confirm His Word to us so that we will continue to value His voice.

When the time came for me to transition from my role in my current church, God miraculously provided as I stepped out in faith to obey the word God had spoken. God continued to speak to me as I prayed about the name of the church and the timing of its planting. God put the name "Gateway" on my heart, and then confirmed it through Genesis 28:17. God continued to teach me about the value of His voice by giving several other confirmations about the church's name. Then the Lord spoke to my wife, Debbie, and me that we should have the first worship service on Easter Sunday. Jimmy Evans, who helped plant the church as a part of Trinity Fellowship, also received confirmation from God about Easter. Then, during a meeting about prophecy, another confirmation came through a prophetic word about Easter. God continued to give many more confirmations in a variety of ways. Gateway Church was not a man's idea; it came from God through multiple confirmations and in many different ways. God will teach us to value His voice. Even if we can hear Him, he wants us to learn from Him and depend upon Him. God is in charge and in control and the more we hear from Him and learn to value His voice, the more He will get the glory for everything.

As you learn to hear and value God's voice, you should first develop the habit of coming to Him on a consistent basis. When you are used to hearing God's general will through His Word and your regular prayer time, you will find it easier to hear a specific word from Him. If you have a job change, buy a new home, or face an important decision, then you want a specific word from the Lord. If you do not have a habit of meeting with and hearing from Him on a regular basis, then you will find it more difficult to hear a specific word. In order to cultivate and value hearing God's voice, you must first set an appointment to meet with Him. Schedule time with God as part of your daily routine.

We arrange our schedules around what is the most important to us. We set a time for things that we don't want to miss. When we schedule time with God, it prioritizes Him. In Exodus, when God was going to meet with Moses and the Israelites, God set a specific time. God wanted the people ready for meeting with Him. He comes to a prepared people in a prepared atmosphere. The Bible contains a pattern of people preparing before coming to God. Even today, we prepare with church services. Many people must prepare for a successful church service. The preparations help to create an atmosphere of expectation. This same principle holds true for us. If we set an appointment to meet with God and come with an expectant heart, we are much more likely to hear His voice. No one else needs to determine your time for meeting with God. Set a time that works for you. Some people prefer mornings and others, evenings. A consistent place is also helpful. Find a place where you can have solitude and focus with minimal distractions. Every person will have a different preference, but the key is to make an appointment to meet with God.

When your appointment begins, be still before God and worship. You may find it challenging to be still and quiet your mind. God encourages people throughout Scripture to wait on Him, to be still, and set their focus. Sometimes they faced difficult battles or situations, just as we do today; we should be still and come to God in the same way. God also instructs people throughout Scripture during worship. As we become still and worship God, our posture helps us hear from the Holy Spirit and engage in meaningful dialogue with Him. After worshipping, pray and read the Bible. Pray from your heart. Don't worry about following a specific pattern or feel as though you need to cover a list. Simply pray for the things on your heart and mind. Also, when you read the Bible, it doesn't matter where you read, as long as you read!

Finally, listen and write what God says to you through prayer or the Scriptures. Many people have developed their ability to hear God through writing. Over time, you will learn to discern God's voice. The discipline of writing will aid you as you review God's direction over time. Writing also requires intentionality and discipline. As you prioritize connecting with God and discerning His general will, you will ready yourself to hear a specific word from Him.

Group Opener

If you could learn and become an expert on any subject, what would it be and why?

Group Talk

1. How do you show people that they are valuable to you?

. . . .
. . . .
. . . .

2. Why do you think it is important to set an appointment to meet with God?

. . . .
. . . .
. . . .

Key Scriptures

Now in the morning, having risen a long while before day-light, He went out and departed to a solitary place; and there He prayed (Mark 1:35).

> I rise before the dawning of the morning,
> And cry for help;
> I hope in Your word (Psalm 119:147).

As you read these verses, what is the Holy Spirit saying to you?

. . . .

. . . .

. . . .

Key Questions

1. Do you find it difficult or easy to meet with God consistently? Why is this your experience? What would be a realistic meeting time and place for your appointments with God?

. . . .

. . . .

. . . .

2. This chapter encourages us to pray about whatever is on our hearts. Why do you think this approach is effective for communicating with God?

. . . .

. . . .

. . . .

Key Responses

1. When you set an appointment to meet with God, follow the pattern described in this chapter: Be still and worship, pray and read, then listen and write. If you miss a day, or even if you miss several days, don't be discouraged. Pick up the habit again. How do you plan to make this practice a habit?

. . . .
. . . .
. . . .

2. If you have never written down your prayers or what you feel like God is saying to you, then begin today. Buy a journal or notebook, or find an effective digital tool that works for you, and begin consistently taking time to listen and write down what God is speaking to you.

. . . .
. . . .
. . . .

CHAPTER SIX

CALL FOR CONFIRMATION

Key Thought

God always confirms His word and it is okay to ask Him for a confirmation. Gideon asked God for several confirmations. God's word to you will always line up with the Bible, agree with godly counsel, and bring peace to your heart.

Summary

Several years ago, the Lord led me and some other ministers to visit the former Yugoslavia to preach. On the way, we had a close encounter with some security guards at a checkpoint. The country was in civil war, creating great instability. After the incident, I needed a clear confirmation from God that He had in fact called us to minister there and would keep us safe. As we began to pray, God put several Scriptures on my heart and spoke a confirming word. After the word from the Lord, I knew that God had indeed commissioned us and was holding us safe in His hands. This confirming word from the Lord brought peace, comfort, and reassurance. It is okay to ask

God to confirm His word to you if you believe He has told you something. The great news is that God always confirms His word. Many times, the Scriptures attest to the fact that God always confirms His word. God understands and endorses the power of confirmation.

The story of Gideon contains many examples of God confirming His word. Many people are familiar with Gideon's fleece. But the whole process of Gideon's journey is full of examples of the gracious way God confirms His word. When the Lord initially appeared to Gideon and commissioned him to lead Israel to defeat the Midianites, the first thing Gideon did was to ask for a confirmation. After spending time preparing an offering, Gideon brought it out to the Lord. God is patient and will wait for us. When Gideon presented the offering and set it on a rock, fire came out of the rock and consumed it. God confirmed His word to Gideon.

After this amazing experience, God again spoke to Gideon and this is where the famous story of the fleece takes place. Gideon laid out a fleece, and in the morning, the ground was dry, but the fleece was so wet it contained an entire bowl full of water. God honored Gideon's request for a confirmation. In fact, the next night, he asked for the opposite to take place and, in the morning, the fleece was dry and the ground around it was wet.

When Gideon finally had an army assembled, God told him to release everyone in the army who was afraid. When two thirds of the army left and he only had ten thousand soldiers, God gave him another test to make the army even smaller. God wanted Israel to know that it wasn't by their might or power that they were delivered, but only the hand of God could save them. God directed Gideon to have the men drink water from the river.

Gideon separated those who drank the water directly from the river from those who drank from their hands. Gideon chose a small group of three hundred men who drank from their hands as his final army. Even after God had directed and confirmed His word several times, Gideon still needed one more confirmation. Gideon snuck down to the Midianite camp and overheard them talking. One man shared his dream and another interpreted the dream as God giving the Midianites into Gideon's hand. When Gideon heard this confirmation, he worshipped God.

In the same way God confirmed His word to Gideon, He will confirm it to you. One way you can receive a confirmation is through the Bible. God's voice never disagrees with what the Bible teaches. Sometimes people say that God spoke something to them, but it does not line up with the clear teaching of the Bible. Anything that a person says is guidance but contradicts the Scripture is not really from the Lord. Someone may take a single Scripture out of context or twist one verse for selfish reasons. Even Satan used Bible verses when he tried to tempt Jesus. Knowing the clear teaching and principles of the Bible will help you spot when a single verse is misused.

If you believe God has spoken to you, then submit that word to prayerful counsel. This does not mean to check with several friends until you find someone who agrees with you. And it doesn't mean you have already made up your mind on the decision and you are simply looking for someone to give you permission. Listening to godly counsel is believing you have heard the Lord and will submit that word to godly, trusted Christians who know you and have an active relationship with God. Those people will sincerely pray with you about the matter and offer wise, biblical input. Again, you are not asking them to hear God for you, rather you are hearing God, asking them to make sure you are not off base, and confirming that what you are hearing lines up with the Bible.

In addition, God's voice will bring peace. It always takes faith to follow God, but fear has no part in that experience. If God leads, He will also give peace. Inner peace is one of the greatest confirmations of God's voice. It goes beyond our understanding and is one of the surest ways to know that God is speaking. If you feel uneasy in your heart or have a check in your spirit about something, God is probably not leading you in that direction. The Bible indicates that not only is it okay to ask God for confirmation, but it's also wise to ask Him to confirm His word.

Group Opener

Has something interesting or comical happened to you as you've traveled somewhere?

Group Talk

1. Why do you think God often speaks to us multiple times about the same thing and is willing to give us so many confirmations?

. . . .

. . . .

. . . .

2. Has God ever spoken to you about something and then confirmed it either one or more times? What did God speak to you, and how did He confirm it?

. . . .
. . . .
. . . .

3. Why is it critical to check everything you believe God is speaking with the Bible's teaching? What dangers exist if you bypass this practice?

. . . .
. . . .
. . . .

4. When you're looking for confirmation, what is the difference between godly counsel and merely asking for the thoughts and opinions of others?

. . . .
. . . .
. . . .

5. Describe a time you had to make a decision. Did you have peace about it or not? Looking back, what can you learn about the way God puts peace in your heart when He is leading you?

. . . .
. . . .
. . . .

Prayer

Heavenly Father, thank You for your patience with us when we ask You for confirmation. Help us always to look to the Bible for confirmation. Please reveal to us those people who can offer godly counsel for us. Thank You for always leading us with Your peace that passes understanding. In Jesus' name, Amen.

Explore

Want to go deeper? Here is some food for thought, prayer, and journaling in the coming week.

Key Quote

God waited for Gideon. And God will wait for us too. God didn't condemn Gideon for wanting confirmation—rather, the opposite of that is true ... God will wait for us to figure out that He's truly talking to us.

—Robert Morris

- One of God's attributes is patience. When you think about your journey of learning to hear God, how have you experienced His patience?

. . . .
. . . .
. . . .

- Describe a time when God has shown patience to you. How do you feel knowing that God wants to walk patiently with you in your relationship with Him?

. . . .
. . . .
. . . .

Key Scripture

Then he said to Him, "If now I have found favor in Your sight, then show me a sign that it is You who talk with me" (Judges 6:17).

As you read this verse, what is the Holy Spirit saying to you?

. . . .
. . . .

Key Questions

1. How is learning to hear God like a journey? In what ways has God walked with you in your journey of learning to hear Him? What are some of the key milestones?

. . . .
. . . .

2. Gideon asked God for confirmation, but he eventually had to act. Once God confirms His word, we must take a step of faith. When have you had to step in faith after God confirmed a word He spoke to you?

. . . .
. . . .

Key Responses:

1. After pressing in to hear God about something, ask Him to confirm His word. Learn to know God's voice in the many ways He will give confirmation.

. . . .
. . . .
. . . .

2. "So then faith *comes* by hearing, and hearing by the word of God" (Romans 10:17). After God has confirmed His word and you know that He is speaking, step out in faith and do what He says.

. . . .
. . . .
. . . .

CHAPTER SEVEN

BE A STEWARD
OF GOD'S VOICE

Key Thought

When God speaks to us, we must listen closely to the words He says, value them, and then we must act upon them in humility, faith, and obedience.

Summary

The Bible teaches us to be good stewards of everything God has given us. Our time, treasure, talents, and even our future do not belong to us. If we have given our lives to Him, then it is all His and we must be good stewards. This same principle applies to hearing God's voice. Whenever we are faithful stewards with the things He has given us, He blesses us with more. When God speaks to us, if we are faithful with the word He gives us, then He will give us more words. The Bible says that when we hear, He will give us more. We must value God's voice.

We are good stewards of God's voice when we truly listen to Him. He speaks in many ways and always has. Throughout Scripture, God spoke in several ways to people, which remains true today. He speaks to people who seek to hear Him with humble hearts and a willingness to act upon His spoken word. God can speak to us through circumstances, such as when He spoke to Jonah. We practice wisdom by looking at the many circumstances of our lives and then asking honestly for Him to show us what He is saying to us through them. God speaks to us through wise counsel that lines up with Scripture and comes from people who prayerfully seek Him for wisdom and insight. He speaks through peace. God will always lead in peace and we should not move forward without it ruling in our hearts. He can speak through people. The Bible contains examples of God sending wise people to speak. He spoke through dreams and visions in both the Old and New Testaments. God speaks through our thoughts. Not every thought is from Him; some thoughts are our own, and some can even come from the devil. God can speak through natural manifestations; He can make Himself known by nature. He can speak through supernatural manifestations such as He did with Moses at the burning bush. God speaks through the Bible. Scripture is always the way He speaks to us in the general sense that God inspired the words of Scripture. He can also speak to us very specifically through Scripture. And, God can speak to us through a whisper. We often refer to this as His still small voice.

If we are going to hear God's voice, then we need to listen to Him. When we tune into the frequency of heaven and hear His voice, then we can stand in faith and act on what He says. When we respond in humility we are careful stewards of God's voice. Pride and a haughty spirit are not conducive to good stewardship. Sometimes people have closed their ears to God's voice. At other times, people can let the cares of life choke their response to God after they hear Him. The parable of the sower found in the Gospel of Luke cautions us about what and how we hear. We want to be like the good soil and have humble, open hearts when we hear God. When our hearts are good soil, or when we hear with humble hearts, God's word brings forth fruit in our life. In the explanation of this parable, Jesus also warns that if people are not careful then they will lose even what they possess. This parable is both an encouragement and a warning about the condition of our hearts when we receive God's words.

When Joseph received a dream from God that his brothers would bow down to him one day, his initial response was prideful and he told his brothers. This prideful response caused envy and brought Joseph trouble. Similarly, we need to be humble stewards when God speaks to us. Thankfully, as Joseph grew up, God did a lot of work in his heart. God can redeem any mistake. When we hear from God, it is important not to use God's words to make ourselves look better. Pride causes all types of problems, but when we are humble, we receive grace. Guard against pride, and always cultivate humility.

As we heed God's words, we become careful stewards of His voice. When Jonah heard God speak, he turned the other way. We can learn from Jonah's wrong response to God's word. God used the natural circumstances of a storm to get Jonah's attention again. In a similar way, if we have heard God speak to us in the past, but we are currently not hearing anything, it is a good idea to go back to the last thing we remember God telling us. If we have not yet done what He asked, or if we have not responded to the last word He spoke, we have an opportunity to repent. In the same way that Jonah repented and then obeyed God, we need to repent when we have not obeyed God, and then turn and obey. Obedience is very important in the life of a believer. We show that we love God by obeying Him. Just as a good surfer must align himself with the power of the ocean, we need to align ourselves with God and yield ourselves to His will and power.

When we are careful stewards of God's voice, we are blessed, but even more, we bless the Lord. Many Psalms are about blessing the Lord. When we handle His word with care, we can actually minister to the Lord. In the book of Acts, before God spoke to the disciples about sending Paul and Barnabas on their specific assignments, they were ministering to the Lord. A correlation exists between ministering to the Lord and the Lord speaking. When we listen to His voice and respond with careful stewardship, we bless Him. We tend to think of stewardship as managing time and money, but Jesus' warning in the Gospel of Mark is that we are responsible to steward God's spoken word as well. Those who listen to God—receive His word with humble hearts and act upon it—will hear God again.

Group Opener

Think about a time when someone did not listen to your words. What emotions did you feel when you were ignored?

Group Talk

1. When you think of the word "stewardship," what comes to your mind? What are some characteristics of a person who is a good steward?

. . . .

. . . .

. . . .

2. What are some things in your life that have value? How do you treat those things? How would you show that you value God's voice?

. . . .

. . . .

. . . .

3. This chapter addresses several ways that God speaks. In which of these ways has He spoken to you, and which of these have you never experienced? If God spoke to you in a way you didn't expect, how would you respond?

. . . .

. . . .

. . . .

4. Why do you think God resists the proud? Why do you think He gives grace to the humble? Why is it important to stay humble when God speaks to you?

. . . .

. . . .

. . . .

5. How does obedience to God's words demonstrate that we value His voice?

. . . .

. . . .

. . . .

Prayer

Heavenly Father, we value Your voice. Thank You for the many ways You speak to us. Help our hearts to be good soil when You speak. Help us to stay humble as You speak to us and help us be obedient to Your word. We want our lives to bless You as we value Your voice. In Jesus' name, Amen.

Explore

Want to go deeper? Here is some food for thought, prayer, and journaling in the coming week.

Key Quote

God is speaking all the time, but the only ones who hear are those who tune in to the right frequency through humility and obedience.

—Robert Morris

- What are some ways you can prepare your heart in humility to tune in to God's voice?

. . . .

. . . .

. . . .

- When have you heard God speak to you and you responded in obedience? Describe that experience.

. . . .
. . . .
. . . .

Key Scriptures

As they ministered to the Lord and fasted, the Holy Spirit said, "Now separate to Me Barnabas and Saul for the work to which I have called them" (Acts 13:2).

Then He said, "Go out, and stand on the mountain before the Lord." And behold, the Lord passed by, and a great and strong wind tore into the mountains and broke the rocks in pieces before the Lord, *but* the Lord *was* not in the wind; and after the wind an earthquake, *but* the Lord *was* not in the earthquake; and after the earthquake a fire, *but* the Lord *was* not in the fire; and after the fire a still small voice (1 Kings 19:11–12).

As you read these verses, what is the Holy Spirit saying to you?

. . . .
. . . .
. . . .

Key Questions

1. What is one of the most challenging things God has ever spoken to you? What made it so challenging?

. . . .
. . . .
. . . .

2. What are some ways you have been a good steward of God's voice in the past? What are some practical ways you plan to steward God's voice when He speaks to you in the future?

. . . .
. . . .
. . . .

Key Responses

1. Has God spoken something to you that you haven't obeyed? If so, your next step of being a good steward is to obey His word. If you have not heard God in a while, He may be waiting for you to respond to the last thing He spoke to you.

. . . .
. . . .
. . . .

2. Bless the Lord. In your response to Him, in the way you value His voice, and in the way you steward what He speaks to you, always respond to God in a way that blesses Him. Ask yourself if you are blessing Him by the way you value His voice.

. . . .
. . . .
. . . .

CHAPTER EIGHT

RECOGNIZE GOD'S VOICE THROUGH RELATIONSHIP

Key Thought

When God is our highest priority, when we pursue Him, and when we are passionate about our relationship with Him, we will recognize His voice.

Summary

Learning to hear God is a journey. It is a process of learning to discern when God is actually speaking to us. God wants us to approach Him with the confidence and knowledge that we truly can hear Him. Although we may feel as though we are in a constant struggle, we can take courage in the clear message of Scripture that we can hear His voice. So, don't give up if you are still learning. The key to hearing the Lord regularly is to grow in your relationship with Him. Jesus paid for all of your sins, so you can confidently come to God. When you come to Him, He will teach you to hear His voice. You know that you can come to God because He has forgiven all your sins. You have also been reconciled to God. Reconciliation means that He puts things back together again. Although at one time we were all far from God, He has forgiven all our sins and brought us into a harmonious relationship. We are not just in right standing with God, but we have the privilege of knowing and talking with Him.

The story of the prodigal in the Gospel of Luke depicts a father who not only forgives his son, but also opens his arms wide and embraces the child. God acts that way toward us. He embraces us, clothes us, calls us His child, and throws a party because we are a part of His family. The truth of the gospel is that God loves us deeply and intensely. He has welcomed us home with open arms and given us so many spiritual blessings.

As we deepen our personal relationship with God, we can hear His voice more clearly. This relationship happens because we are able to recognize His voice more easily. As it grows, we become more familiar with Him and His voice. On our journey of getting to know and hear God, sometimes we don't hear him. This too is normal. Abraham heard God, yet there are long stretches of time, sometimes several years, where Genesis records nothing about God speaking to him. God highly favored Job, but He did not speak to him until the very end of Job's difficult trials. Even as we develop our relationship with God, we may still experience these times. However, in general, the closer our relationship with God, the better we can hear His voice.

We should consider our relationship with God our highest priority. Jesus invites us to follow Him closely, so that we can exchange the superficial pleasures of sin for the true, deep, and lasting pleasures of knowing Him. Satan tries to get us to believe the lie that sin will bring us pleasure, peace, joy, and fulfillment. But following his lies only causes us to lose what we already have. We don't lose our salvation, but we will lose our close fellowship with God. That is what happened to Adam and Eve. At first, they would meet and talk with God daily. They spent time with Him and had sweet fellowship and communion. After Adam and Eve disobeyed God and sinned, rather than having their normal time of being together, they hid from Him. They were afraid and even feared God's voice. Sin changed everything in their relationship. The good news is that Jesus came to restore the relationship and cancel the effects of sin. Now, our goal is to make our relationship with God our highest priority, so that we can be dead to sin and alive to Christ.

We must also make our relationship with God our highest pursuit. When we pursue something, we run after and strive for it with all our might. In the garden of Eden, Adam and Eve sinned when they ate from the tree of knowledge of good and evil. But God put another tree in the garden that they could eat from—the tree of life. God wanted them to live in such a way that they weren't always trying to decide between good and evil. His intention was that they would eat life—that they would live by His voice. When Satan tempted them, he was trying to get them to doubt God's voice. God does not want us to attempt to determine good from evil and use our conscience to make choices. When we make our decisions based on His voice, they are based on life. When we make decisions based on only our conscience, we can still be led astray. It is possible to have a seared conscience, or one that doesn't align with God's Word. The best thing a conscience can do is tell us what's good and bad and convict us of sin, so that we know we need Jesus as our Savior. If our conscience makes us aware that we have done something wrong, the Holy Spirit will come in and bring Godly conviction that will lead us to salvation. Some people try to use their conscience as a guide, but they will find themselves doing dead works to gain God's favor because they feel bad. Instead, the Bible makes it clear that the blood of Jesus cleanses our conscience from dead works. When we follow Christ, the Holy Spirit who lives inside of us convicts us of right and wrong, rather than our conscience. The Bible does tell us to keep our conscience pure, but it always emphasizes hearing and obeying His voice.

Our relationship with God must be our highest passion. When we are passionate about God, He stirs our highest feelings of love and devotion. In Luke 10 when Jesus was having dinner with Mary and Martha, Martha was busy working, but Mary sat at His feet. Mary was passionate about being with Jesus, spending time with Him, and listening to Him. Martha was troubled and worried about her to-do list. When we are passionate about Jesus, we take the time to lay down all our busy activities and simply spend time with Him.

God desires for us to have such a deep, intimate relationship with Him that we would know His voice, and even sense the deep things of His heart. When human relationships are close, we don't even need words to communicate. God wants to have this level of intimacy with us. When we make God our priority, and pursue Him with passion, we will learn to hear His voice because of our deep relationship with Him.

Group Opener

In high school, what was your highest priority, or greatest pursuit?

Group Talk

1. What does it look like to make our relationship with God a priority?

....
....
....

2. What things normally compete for first place in your life?

....
....
....

3. How can you practically pursue God and keep your passion for Him?

....
....
....

4. In the story from Luke 10 about Mary and Martha, which character do you identify with more? Explain your answer.

....
....
....

5. What are your biggest hindrances to developing an intimate relationship with God?

....
....
....

Prayer

Heavenly Father, we are so thankful that You have forgiven us and also reconciled us to Yourself. We are so thankful that Jesus made a way to restore our relationship with You. We want to make our relationship with You our top priority. We want to pursue you with passion. Help us as we learn to hear Your voice and grow in our relationship with You. In Jesus' name, Amen.

Explore

Want to go deeper? Here is some food for thought, prayer, and journaling in the coming week.

Key Quote

We can recognize the voice of God when we are in a deep relationship with Him. The depth of our relationship with God is the foundation for knowing His voice.

—Robert Morris

- How does a deeper relationship help you to have greater recognition of God's voice? What does God's voice usually sound like to you? What have you learned about Him and your relationship with Him as He has spoken to you?

. . . .
. . . .
. . . .

- What are some aspects or characteristics of God's voice that you have learned as you've grown in your relationship with Him? What have you learned about God's voice from reading the Bible?

....
....
....

Key Scriptures

For if when we were enemies we were reconciled to God through the death of His Son, much more, having been reconciled, we shall be saved by His life. And not only *that*, but we also rejoice in God through our Lord Jesus Christ, through whom we have now received the reconciliation (Romans 5:10–11).

Draw near to God and He will draw near to you. Cleanse *your* hands, *you* sinners; and purify *your* hearts, *you* double-minded (James 4:8).

But seek first the kingdom of God and His righteousness, and all these things shall be added to you (Matthew 6:33).

As you read these verses, what is the Holy Spirit saying to you?

....
....
....

Key Questions

1. There is a difference between the tree of life and the tree of knowledge of good and evil. How do you know when you

are living by the knowledge of good and evil as opposed to when you are living according to the tree of life?

. . . .
. . . .
. . . .

2. What is the difference between living by God's voice and living according to your conscience?

. . . .
. . . .
. . . .

Key Responses

1. Take time to think about what it looks like for you to prioritize, pursue, and have passion about your relationship with God. What things normally stand in your way? How can you overcome those things so that you can develop a deeper relationship with God?

. . . .
. . . .
. . . .

2. Ask God to show you where you live either by your conscience or by your own knowledge of good and evil or by pursuing life. Ask Him to help you live by His Spirit in accordance with His life.

. . . .
. . . .
. . . .

CHAPTER NINE

HEAR GOD'S VOICE
FOR OTHERS

Key Thought

All believers can prophesy because we can all hear God. God wants to speak to us so that we can encourage, edify, and comfort others. He wants us to pursue love and to desire spiritual gifts, especially so that we may prophesy.

Summary

As you learn to hear and recognize God's voice, there will be times He will speak to you, so that you can encourage, edify, or comfort others. This practice is called prophecy. Sometimes believers become concerned when they hear the word *prophecy* because there have been abuses of the concept and there is more than one way the word can be applied. Some of these concerns are justified because some people have said they have a gift of prophecy or a prophetic word, but when they share, it is not in line with Scripture, or is discouraging, disruptive, or even plain weird. Some people have even made a big show and have appeared on television or on the news with doom and gloom messages about the destruction of the world on a particular date. Then the day comes and goes and nothing happens. Although some people may act weird, and there are times when someone will give what they say is a prophecy, but it really isn't, it does not discount what the Bible teaches about a healthy, balanced, and very encouraging gift.

The Bible does warn about false prophets and both the Old Testament and New Testament caution us to watch out. Some people might look, sound, or do good things on the surface, but if what they're saying isn't in line with the gospel of Jesus Christ or the rest of the Bible, then we should beware of them. If we put these abuses aside, we can look at what the Bible teaches regarding this spiritual gift.

In the more general sense of the word, prophecy is an encouraging message from the Lord that we give to someone. A prophet is someone who speaks and teaches the words of God. In this sense, a pastor or leader who opens his Bible and preaches from God's revealed Word is a prophet. In this sense also, a Christian whom the Holy Spirit prompts to speak or act in a certain way has received the gift of prophecy. The New Testament often uses this broader sense of the word prophecy and makes it clear that today we should evaluate a prophet's words because they do not stand on the same level as the inspired Scripture. Paul says, "Let two or three prophets speak, and let the others judge" (1 Corinthians 14:29). Scripture is also clear that prophets can be both men and women. In Acts, Philip the evangelist had four unmarried daughters who prophesied, and the early church blessed and welcomed this function.

All Christians can hear God for the edification of others. When we receive the Holy Spirit, He is not silent. He wants to have an intimate, communicative relationship with us. As we walk with Him, He will speak to us and give us words or impressions that encourage others. This is different and needs to be clearly distinguished from the gift of prophecy that Paul mentions in Ephesians 4. There he writes about apostles, prophets, evangelists, pastors, and teachers who have specific ministry gifts, which are used to equip the saints so that they can engage in ministry. Every believer needs to evangelize and share the gospel with others, but some believers have a specific ministry of evangelism. This pattern is also true for the gift of prophecy. Some believers have this specific ministry gift, but we can all hear God and give encouraging or comforting words to others. Moses gathered seventy men, the Spirit of the Lord rested on them, and they prophesied. But after the spirit of the Lord left, they never prophesied again. They used the gift, but did not have that specific gift (Numbers 11). Paul tells the Corinthians to "pursue love, and desire spiritual *gifts*, but especially that you may prophesy" (1 Corinthians 14:1). Why would Paul say to do that if not all believers could do it? All Christians can hear God for the edification of others.

Prophecy is never manipulative. Unfortunately, some individuals have given their own opinion or expressed something from their own hearts and attached the words: "The Lord said ...." When this happens, what is taking place is not true prophecy, but rather manipulation. Scripture gives strong warnings for those who misuse the name of God in this manner. Several times in the Old Testament God strongly rebukes people who say the Lord spoke something, when God in fact didn't speak that way. When the third commandment tells us not to use the name of the Lord in vain, it includes not only using His name in a profane way, but it also means that we are not to use His name for our own vain, selfish reasons. Too many times unhealthy people have tried to get their way or expressed their own selfish desires and attached God's name to it as an attempt to get others to do what they want. One important factor about words from the Lord is that they need confirmation. God will always confirm His word to you—especially if it pertains to something significant in your life. God does not bring confusion, but He always brings peace.

God is concerned about our motives and attitudes when we share with people. Prophecy builds people up; it doesn't tear them down. Paul clearly states, "He who prophesies speaks edification and exhortation and comfort to men" (1 Corinthians 14:3). A simple way to judge if a prophecy is from God is to ask if it brings encouragement, exhortation, or comfort. Prophecy occurs so that all may learn the words and intentions of God. Barnabas was an encourager. His real name was Joses, but he was such an encourager that the disciples gave him the name Barnabas, which means "Son of Encouragement." A person who prophesies acts like Barnabas (an encourager). If you have ever had a thought to call someone or send a note or an encouraging card, it is possible that you are hearing God. The devil will not tell you to encourage someone, but God will. Sometimes the Holy Spirit will even prompt your heart simply to pray for the encouragement of someone.

The Holy Spirit dwells within us and guides us into all truth. He does not want to be silent; He wants to have an intimate, communicative relationship with us. As we walk with Him, He will speak to us and give us words. Sometimes these words will be for us; at other times, these words will be for the edification, exhortation, or comfort of others.

Group Opener

Share about a time when someone did or said something and you felt encouraged or comforted.

Group Talk

1. What thoughts, words, or images come to your mind when you hear the word *prophecy*? Are they generally positive, negative, or neutral? Why do you think these things come to your mind?

. . . .
. . . .
. . . .

2. Why do you think so many people misunderstand prophecy?

. . . .
. . . .
. . . .

3. What are some ways to know if a prophetic word is correct? What are some ways a prophetic word might be confirmed?

. . . .
. . . .
. . . .

4. Has anyone ever given you a prophetic word that was encouraging? What was it?

. . . .

. . . .

5. Why is it important to know God as an encouraging Father when you seek spiritual gifts, especially prophetic words?

. . . .

. . . .

Prayer

Heavenly Father, thank You for speaking to us in love. Lord, help us to hear Your voice clearly so that we may encourage others with prophetic words. We seek You and ask You to give us spiritual gifts, especially the gift of prophecy. In Jesus' name, Amen.

Explore

Want to go deeper? Here is some food for thought, prayer, and journaling in the coming week.

Key Quote

When we receive the Holy Spirit—and when we yield our lives to Him, and He fills and influences our lives—He walks alongside us, encouraging us, guiding us, leading us, assuring us .... As we walk with Him, He will speak to us and give us words or impressions that encourage others.

—Robert Morris

- What role does yielding your life to the Holy Spirit play in your ability to hear God for other people?

. . . .
. . . .

- How does the Holy Spirit encourage, guide, lead, and assure you? How does recognizing the way He encourages you to help you to encourage others more accurately?

. . . .
. . . .

Key Scriptures

Pursue love, and desire spiritual gifts, but especially that you may prophesy (1 Corinthians 14:1).

But he who prophesies speaks edification and exhortation and comfort to men (1 Corinthians 14:3).

As you read these verses, what is the Holy Spirit saying to you?

. . . .
. . . .

Key Questions

1. Do you desire spiritual gifts, especially the gift of prophecy? If no, what are some of the reasons that you don't? If

yes, what have you asked God for and how have you cultivated your ability to hear Him clearly for someone else's encouragement?

. . . .

. . . .

2. Why do you think God would want His people to cultivate and use the gift of prophecy?

. . . .

. . . .

Key Responses

1. Pray for someone who is on your heart. Ask God to show you how to speak to you about that person. As He speaks to you or as you feel a direction of how to pray, begin to pray that way. This is a good way to develop and grow in prophecy. You don't even need to tell that person. Just praying will help you hear God's heart for others.

. . . .

. . . .

2. Stretch your faith as God speaks to you about ways to encourage others. Ask Him to confirm that you are hearing Him correctly. When you receive a confirmation, take a step of faith and encourage someone. You don't have to tell that person it is a prophetic word; you can simply offer encouragement by sharing something.

. . . .

. . . .

CHAPTER TEN

HEAR GOD'S VOICE
FOR A BREAKTHROUGH

Key Thought

Often in our lives, we need a clear, specific word from God so we can experience breakthrough. When God speaks, we can respond with faith and obedience to what He says.

Summary

Often, we need a specific word from God so that we can stand on faith and receive a breakthrough. We experience many situations and circumstances where this is the case. We may be praying for a breakthrough with an issue related to our family, finances, or relationships. Maybe we need a breakthrough in an area of spiritual freedom, or we want fresh perspective and spiritual understanding about a difficult time or event in our lives. We all encounter times when we need a specific word from God. We long to hear His voice clearly. A breakthrough in our lives may be God bringing a complete solution to a problem, or it may be that the problem no longer has the same weight as it did before. Sometimes God breaks through and gives us insight, faith, hope, or resolve. He gives us breakthroughs in many ways, but they are always perfect for the situation and timing of what we are facing. God is love, and He responds to us in exactly the way we need, even if it is different from our original expectation.

King David gives great insight into God's strategy for breakthrough. When he faced an enemy, David's default response was to inquire of the Lord. In his need for a breakthrough, he would first turn and talk to God. When David heard a word from the Lord, he then knew with certainty that he would be victorious. In the same way, when we encounter a difficult situation and need a breakthrough—regardless of the reason—our first response should always be to turn to the Lord. Sometimes God will speak to us through a specific passage of Scripture, and other times He will speak to our hearts by a nudging or His still small voice whispering to us.

If we define faith as taking God at His word, then we need to have a word from God that we can believe in and act upon. Once God tells us what to do, we are not moving on presumption and we have faith to act. We can't act with confidence and faith until we are certain that God has spoken to us. It is worth the time to seek God and press into Him.

When King David inquired of the Lord, he did not do it because he was inexperienced or incapable of battle. David was more than capable and had experienced victory over the enemy many times before. But he also knew that a much greater strength and confidence would come from relying on God. Relying on God is better than any human strategy or tactic. When we are faced with difficulty in life, it is God's voice to us, not human strategy that will bring the breakthrough we seek. We will not have breakthroughs in our lives unless we have faith. And we will not have faith unless we hear God. Therefore, we will not have any breakthroughs unless we purposely and regularly set aside time to hear from God. Faith is never blind. Faith always relies upon God's voice. Once we hear God, we can have true faith.

The place in our lives where the enemy thinks he's the strongest is the exact place where God desires to give us breakthroughs. He is the master of breakthroughs. God will give you a victory in the exact area where you don't think you can have a breakthrough. But faith by itself is not enough. Works accompany true faith. When God speaks and gives us faith, we must then couple works with that faith, step out, and do something about it. If we only hear and believe, but then sit down and don't respond, nothing will happen. Good works are an expression, or evidence, of our faith. When King David went out to fight against the Philistines, even though he had already defeated them once before, he still inquired of God. This time, God gave him a different strategy to win the battle. So, David obeyed. When God gives us a word, and we put our faith into action, this is also called obedience. When we inquire of the Lord and He directs our paths straight, then we need to run in the direction of those straight paths. Obedience is simply doing what God tells you to do. A wise man hears God's word and obeys it, while a foolish man hears God's word, but does whatever he wants. The difference between the wise and the foolish is obedience.

In the area where you are praying and asking God for a breakthrough, you must align yourself with the direction God wants you to go and then walk down that path. It takes listening to God and then obeying Him. This is how faith and actions go together to bring about a breakthrough. God is always speaking to us. He loves us and desires communication with us. When we need to hear a word from God, whether we are in a difficult situation or not, we need to seek God and listen for Him. Sometimes breakthrough takes intentionality and time. When God does speak, we need to respond appropriately. Sometimes when God speaks, He gives us a breakthrough by showing us a new perspective. Other times, He may lead us in a completely new direction. Either way, once we hear God, we need to activate our faith by responding in obedience. The more we respond to His voice and to the nudges in our heart, the more He will speak and we will hear. God did not lose His voice two thousand years ago. In the same way He spoke all throughout the Bible, He still speaks today. He desires for us to know Him and to walk with Him in a relationship that is full of healthy communication. When He speaks, listen and obey. It is an amazing privilege to know the God of the universe personally. We are His sheep and can hear His voice.

Group Opener

What is the best advice anyone has ever given to you? How has it influenced your life?

Group Talk

1. Can you think of a time in your life when you needed a breakthrough and God gave you the perfect word for your situation? What was that experience like?

. . . .

. . . .

. . . .

2. How does hearing a specific word from God fill your heart with faith?

. . . .
. . . .
. . . .

3. What is the difference between presumption and acting in faith?

. . . .
. . . .
. . . .

4. Why do you think the Bible says faith without works is dead? Why does true faith require action?

. . . .
. . . .
. . . .

5. What encouragement would you give to someone who needed to hear God for a breakthrough?

. . . .
. . . .
. . . .

Prayer

Heavenly Father, thank You for Your love and concern for us. Thank You for speaking words to us that are specific to the situations we are facing. We ask that You would give us breakthroughs in our lives. When You speak to us, give us faith and courage to act and respond in obedience to what You tell us. We invite You into every area of our lives. In Jesus' name, Amen.

Explore

Want to go deeper? Here is some food for thought, prayer, and journaling in the coming week.

Key Quote

Faith is never to be flung out into a void; faith must have God's word to stand on.

—Robert Morris

- Describe a time when God spoke something specific to you and it gave you faith to stand.

. . . .
. . . .
. . . .

- Have you ever heard God speak to you, but you didn't respond with faith? What was the situation? How do you plan to respond in the future when God speaks?

. . . .
. . . .
. . . .

Key Scriptures

Thus also faith by itself, if it does not have works, is dead.
But someone will say, "You have faith, and I have works."
Show me your faith without your works, and I will show you my
faith by my works. You believe that there is one God. You do well.
Even the demons believe—and tremble! But do you want to know,
O foolish man, that faith without works is dead? (James 2:17–20).

For by grace you have been saved through faith, and that not
of yourselves; *it is* the gift of God, not of works, lest anyone should
boast. For we are His workmanship, created in Christ Jesus for good
works, which God prepared beforehand that we should walk in them
(Ephesians 2:8–10).

As you read these verses, what is the Holy Spirit saying to you?

. . . .

. . . .

. . . .

Key Questions

1. Why is a specific word from God necessary to have faith for
   a specific breakthrough?

. . . .

. . . .

. . . .

2. What are some specific breakthroughs you would like to
   see in your life?

. . . .
. . . .
. . . .

Key Responses

1. Think about your response to the previous question. Take time to ask God for a specific word from Him concerning an area of your life where you want to see a breakthrough. You may need to seek God through prayer and fasting. Be tenacious and persistent to press in and hear God.

. . . .
. . . .
. . . .

2. If God has spoken to you about an area of your life, and you've had faith, but have not yet taken action, now is the time. Don't simply listen to God's voice and do nothing. Let your faith come alive as you step out and have works. It will bring God glory when your faith is activated. How will you step out in faith?

. . . .
. . . .
. . . .

HOW TO USE THE CURRICULUM

This curriculum has a simple design and can be used for study by individuals, small groups, or in a combination. The following features will help you as you read the book:

Key Thought

This is a brief description under each chapter title that summarizes the main point—the key idea—of the chapter.

Summary

Although each person is encouraged to read the whole chapter before this study, the summary is helpful for a quick review. If you use this material in a small group, it is a quick guide you can use to refresh your thoughts.

Group Opener

This is an ice-breaker question that is usually more light-hearted. The intent is to allow people to become comfortable talking. The questions are also designed to foster relationships as they help the group members get to know each other.

Group Talk

If you are using this material as a part of a small group, these questions are geared toward small group discussion. They are meant to engage each person and generate helpful dialogue around the content of the chapters.

Prayer

Pray together. If you have time, encourage group members to share their prayer concerns.

Key Quote

This is a quote from Pastor Robert Morris, which presents a key idea from each chapter. Questions follow the quote, and these can either be discussed by the group or used for individual study and reflection.

Key Scriptures

If you are using this material for individual study, these Scriptures relate to the content of the chapter and allow for further reflection and application. You may also use them for small group discussion.

Key Questions

You may respond to these questions before or after the small group, but they are geared toward personal reflection. At times, a group leader may find it helpful or appropriate to ask one of these questions in the larger group.

Key Responses

This section encourages personal reflection. They should be considered for journaling, prayer, or further action.

KEY TIPS
FOR THE LEADER

- Generate participation and discussion.
- Resist the urge to teach. The goal is to encourage great conversation that leads to discovery.
- Ask open-ended questions—questions that can't be answered with "yes" or "no" (e.g., "What do you think about that?" rather than "Do you agree?")
- When a question arises, ask the group for input instead of providing your own answer.
- Be comfortable with silence. If you ask a question and no one responds, rephrase the question and wait for a response. Your primary role is to create an environment where people feel comfortable to be themselves and participate, not to provide the answers to all of their questions.
- Ask the group members to pray for each other during the week, especially about key issues that arise during your group discussion. This is how you begin to build authentic community and encourage spiritual growth within the group.

KEYS TO A DYNAMIC SMALL GROUP

Relationships

Meaningful, encouraging relationships are the foundation of a dynamic small group. Teaching, discussion, worship, and prayer are important elements of a group meeting, but the depth of each element often depends upon the depth of the relationships between the group members.

Availability

Building a sense of community within your group requires members to prioritize their relationships with one another. This means being available to listen, care for one another, and meet each other's needs.

Mutual Respect

Mutual respect is shown when members value others' opinions (even when they disagree) and take care to never belittle or embarrass others in the group (including their spouses, who may or may not be present).

Openness

A healthy small group environment encourages sincerity and transparency. Members treat each other with grace in areas of weakness, allowing each other room to grow.

Confidentiality

To develop authenticity and a sense of safety within the group, each member must be able to trust that things discussed within the group will not be shared outside the group.

Shared Responsibility

Group members will share the responsibility of group meetings by using their God-given abilities to serve at each gathering. Some may greet, some may host, some may teach, etc. Ideally, group members should be available to care for one another as needed.

Sensitivity

Dynamic small groups are born when the leader consistently seeks and is responsive to the guidance of the Holy Spirit, following His leading throughout the meeting as opposed to sticking to the "agenda." This practice is especially important during the discussion and ministry time.

Fun!

Dynamic small groups take time to have fun! Create an atmosphere for fun, and be willing to laugh at yourself every now and then!

NOTES

FREQUENCY